CRIES OF FAITH, SONGS OF HOPE

D0048016

CRIES OF FAITH, SONGS OF HOPE

PRAYERS FOR THE TIMES OF OUR LIFE

JOHN GUGEL

STEPHEN MINISTRIES • ST. LOUIS, MO

Cries of Faith, Songs of Hope:
Prayers for the Times of Our Life

ISBN: 1-930445-10-5

Stephen Ministries Permissions Department
2045 Innerbelt Business Center Drive
St. Louis, Missouri 63114-5765

07   06   05   04

4   3   2   1

INTRODUCTION

These prayers have been prayed before. They spring from a pastoral heart and have been prayed at the altar, at hospital bedsides, in counseling sessions, and in a host of other life situations. They also rose from the author's own struggles with chronic, disabling disease.

The prayers in this book are grouped into three parts. A vignette, brief commentary, Scripture passage, or hymn stanza accompanies each prayer to highlight its theme, strengthen its meaning, and give it wings.

Part 1, "Prayers for Christians during Tough Times," was inspired by the scriptural psalms of lament. While these 50 or so psalms are brutally honest in presenting their case to God, they also ring with hope and conclude with a vow to praise God for God's goodness. The prayers in this section seek to capture and emulate that mood and spirit.

They are confrontational and literally storm the gates of heaven with their directness, based on faith.

Part 2, "Prayers from the Heart," covers a smorgasbord of issues in the life of a Christian. The dilemmas of life present issues that require decisions or a faithful response. The prayers in this section seek to put words to human quandaries felt deeply in the heart.

Part 3, "Times and Seasons," includes prayers to be used at different times of the day as well as for seasons of both the secular and liturgical calendars.

My prayer for this book is that it supply you with words you need, with hope, and with a place in the lap of God where you will feel secure.

PART ONE

PRAYERS FOR CHRISTIANS DURING TOUGH TIMES

WHEN IN NEED OF RESCUE

READING

ONE DAY [JESUS] got into a boat with his disciples, and he said to them, "Let us go across to the other side of the lake." So they put out, and while they were sailing he fell asleep. A windstorm swept down on the lake, and the boat was filling with water, and they were in danger. They went to him and woke him up, shouting, "Master, Master, we are perishing!" And he woke up and rebuked the wind and the raging waves; they ceased, and there was a calm. He said to them, "Where is your faith?" They were afraid and amazed, and said to one another, "Who then is this, that he commands even the winds and the water, and they obey him?"

— Luke 8:22–25 (NRSV)

PRAYER

I NEED YOU, LORD. I need your help. I need your hand to hold onto. I feel as if I am sinking in a swirling sea of endless conflict and difficult issues. I have little strength left, and I am weary of the struggle. Reach out to me, Lord. Hear the cry of your servant and come. Just speak the word. Command the wind and the raging waves. Calm the seas and carry me to safe harbor. Do not let the undertow of fear whisk me back out to the dangerous deep. Hold me and keep me as your own for all time and all eternity. I need you, Lord. Do not desert your servant.

FOR EYES TO SEE

READING

A MIGHTY FORTRESS is our God,
A sword and shield victorious;
He breaks the cruel oppressor's rod
And wins salvation glorious.
The old satanic foe
Has sworn to work us woe!
With craft and dreadful might
He arms himself to fight.
On earth he has no equal.[1]

— Martin Luther, 1483–1546

---

1 "A Mighty Fortress Is Our God," stanza 1, hymn 229. Text copyright © 1978 LUTHERAN BOOK OF WORSHIP. Used by permission of Augsburg Fortress.

PRAYER

"LOOK ON the bright side," people tell me, Lord. But I can see only shadows and darkness. I would settle for a silver lining. I would be satisfied with a single sliver of light. A mere glimmer would be enough. Open my eyes, Lord. Help me see your promised salvation. Let me know that there is nothing in heaven or on earth that can ever separate me from your great love. Be my God and my salvation, my fortress and my rock, my hiding place and my eternal home. Shine the light of your grace into the dark corners of my life. Crank up the candlepower. Surround me with your own brilliant light, O God, my bulwark, strong and mighty.

FOR ACCEPTANCE OF GOD'S WILL

READING

WALT HAD successfully climbed the corporate ladder, starting out in the factory, working his way up to vice-president for product development. His days started early in the morning and ended late at night. Lorene dutifully shouldered most of the work of raising their family and maintaining their home. They had great plans for Walt's retirement—travel, golf, and sunny days. That was before the lump appeared. Surgery, chemotherapy, and radiation bought some time but could not stop the tumor's relentless growth. Walt attended to Lorene's every need, fixing her meals, bathing her, changing her bandages, holding her fragile body in his arms for hours to relieve her pain. It was on one of their pastor's visits that Walt told her, "For the first time in our lives we are learning to pray the Lord's Prayer, but we never dreamed it would be this hard."

PRAYER

"THY WILL be done." Why is it so hard to say those words, Lord, and mean them? Why is your will so difficult to accept, let alone be the object of prayer? Why do I find it so hard to trust? Keep me praying, Lord. Do not let my fears and struggles so overwhelm me that your mercy cannot reach me. Let me see your hand at work in my life. Let me know that your will for my life is loving, right, and perfect. When your will seems hard and impossible to accept, let me fall back on my certainty of your love.

FOR RELIEF FROM DEPRESSION

READING

DEPRESSION IS A PROBLEM that affects many people. Some, unfortunately, don't take it seriously enough. They believe it to be a character flaw or a personal weakness. This is too bad. They act as though positive thinking alone would dispel depression. The depressed person who comes to believe this may resist treatment or cut off outside help, full of self-blame for not being strong enough. Again, this is too bad. There are in fact many very effective ways to treat depression.

Caregivers, do not give up on those who may be depressed, but do recognize the need sometimes to refer them for professional care. Sufferers, do not give up on the possibility of help. Help is available.

PRAYER

DARKNESS SURROUNDS ME, Lord, thick, unrelenting, deep darkness. I long to see your face. I eagerly seek your gentle touch. I need to know that you are here for me. Be my light shining in the murky mist, my hope for all seasons, my support in suffering, my strength in weakness, my guide when I am lost. Hold me in your arms—tight but without smothering. Lighten my burden, cheer my sagging spirit, and restore me to your wholeness. Then I will praise your gracious name now and ever.

FOR STRENGTH

READING

S T. PAUL WRITES, "Three times I pleaded with the Lord to take [the thorn in my flesh] away from me. But he said to me, 'My grace is sufficient for you, for my power is made perfect in weakness.' Therefore I will boast all the more gladly about my weaknesses, so that Christ's power may rest on me."

— 2 Corinthians 12:8–9 (NIV)

PRAYER

YOUR LOGIC IS STRANGE, Lord. You say that while I am weak you are strong. That doesn't make any sense. I don't like being weak, dependent, helpless. I want to be in charge of my life. I want to make my own decisions. I want to be confident and strong. Let me see your eternal wisdom. Let me know your kind grace as I put my hand in yours to be led. Help me accept that which I cannot understand, trusting that your grace is supplying my every need.

FOR WHOLENESS

READING

*S*HALOM IS A STURDY Hebrew word. It literally means "peace." But *shalom* has a much broader meaning than just the end of hostilities. It describes the wholeness that God promises for his people. It describes the totality of God's goodness to those who are God's own.

PRAYER

GIVE ME YOUR SHALOM, Lord. Make me whole once more. Mend my brokenness. Restore my fractured spirit. Put the pieces back together again. Set my troubled soul at rest. Hush the turmoil within and soothe me with your own indescribable peace so that I might proclaim your goodness and be an agent of shalom to everyone I encounter.

WHEN LOGIC FAILS

READING

LISA ALWAYS could sense when her daddy was stressed out from work. He would come home in the evening and plop down in his easy chair, exhausted. In a flash Lisa would be standing at his side, a book to read in one hand and her favorite "binkie" in the other. He would lift her onto his lap and cuddle. Within minutes he could feel the tension of work melt away. What did not add up was evidenced by the stocking cap she wore on her head—a reminder of her courageous ongoing battle with cancer. She was so young and so precious. Why, then? Logic failed to provide an answer.

PRAYER

"THERE MUST BE a reason." How easily those words passed from my lips, Lord, when I tried to comfort others in their times of need. How those words haunt me now. There must be a logical explanation, but somehow it escapes me. I long for a reason that makes even a little sense, but it eludes me. What if there is no explanation? I can only handle that, Lord, if you prepare me with your help. I can accept that, but only by your rich grace. I can live with that only if you are at my side. I need your love, Lord—full glass, overflowing, filling every crevice of my mind and every crease of my soul.

WHEN LIFE IS NOT FAIR

READING

WHEN MY SON was three years old and something did not go the way he wanted it to, he was likely to say, "That's not fair!" I would respond in a teasing, flat monotone, "Jeremy, life isn't fair." This happened several times until finally, in desperation, before I could say the words he did not want to hear, he added in a loud voice, ". . . and don't tell me life isn't fair." Jeremy didn't like to hear this particular slice of the truth about life. But then, who among us does?

PRAYER

L IFE IS NOT FAIR, Lord. Why do bad things happen to good people? Why do pain and suffering afflict the faithful? Why do the righteous suffer? Give me an answer. Better yet, stand by me. Keep me faithful in season and out. Restore my life. Do not abandon me to my fears and misgivings, but hold me close in your eternal embrace.

WHEN LIFE IS DIFFICULT

READING

O GIVE THANKS to the LORD, for he is good;
    his steadfast love endures forever! . . .

The LORD is my strength and my might;
    he has become my salvation. . . .

I shall not die, but I shall live,
    and recount the deeds of the LORD. . . .

Open to me the gates of righteousness,
    that I may enter through them
    and give thanks to the LORD.

— Psalm 118:1, 14, 17, and 19 (NRSV)

PRAYER

WHAT DOES the future hold, Lord? What will become of me? Why do I find more questions than answers? Where are you, Lord? Do you care? Send me your Spirit. Give me confidence in your great promises and unwavering hope in your lavish mercy. Let me feel your tender compassion. Be with me, Lord. Lead me into the future where you are. Grant me a living faith and, by the strength of your arm, lighten my load. Cheer my heart, sustain me by your mighty power, and lead me in the paths of your own choosing.

of rightiousness.
Help me to know of your
love for me. Help me to
know my purpose in life.
— May my life be filled with
the joy of knowing your
love for me.

FOR HEALING

READING

M Y GOD IS NOT some Greek god, uninvolved in the world of us humans. My God is Yahweh, the good old Hebrew God who is quite willing to mix it up with us humans, to hear our prayers and answer them. In the story of Lazarus, there is a glimpse of what this means:

> But when Jesus heard it, he said, "This illness does not lead to death; rather it is for God's glory, so that the Son of God may be glorified through it." . . . Jesus said to [Martha], "Did I not tell you that if you believed, you would see the glory of God?"
>
> — John 11:4; 40 (NRSV)

PRAYER

L ET ME be straight with you, Lord. I know you love me, and I know you don't want me to be sick and dying. I know that you are creator of all that is, and therefore able to master it. I want to live, Lord. I want to be well. Heal me, I beg you. I rely on your mercy and love. Even if I must die, I rely on you and your promises. Strengthen me in body and spirit so that I might sing your praises and be a witness for your glory.

WHILE WAITING FOR THE RESULTS OF MEDICAL TESTS

READING

THE WORST PART of Hank's medical tests, he had about decided, was this confounded waiting. Everyone seemed to be taking their sweet time about getting back to him with the results. He sat nervously by the phone, reaching for it to call again and then putting his hands back in his lap where his fingers twisted together without his even being aware of it. He had already called twice today, three times in the last two days. The nurse was still pleasant to him, but he knew he was beginning to seem like a pest. Still, it was his life that was in the balance here.

PRAYER

PATIENCE IS NOT my best feature, Lord. I know you have me in mind, but I'm frightened. I don't want bad news, and I don't want to wait. My mind is racing, Lord. I think of a hundred ways that things can go wrong and can't keep focused on you having me right in the palm of your hand. Help me to accept the results with courage and fortitude, regardless of what they are. Stay by my side now, Lord, and teach me patience, knowing that you have only my good in mind.

ON FACING DEATH

READING

LORD, LET at last thine angels come,
To Abr'hams bosom bear me home,
   That I may die unfearing;
And in its narrow chamber keep
My body safe in peaceful sleep
   Until thy reappearing.
And then from death awaken me,
That these mine eyes with joy may see,
      O Son of God, thy glorious face,
      My Savior and my fount of grace.
Lord Jesus Christ,
My prayer attend, my prayer attend,
And I will praise thee without end![1]

— Martin Schalling, 1532–1608

---

1 "Lord, Thee I Love with All My Heart," stanza 3, hymn 325, from *Lutheran Book of Worship* (Minneapolis: Augsburg Publishing House, 1978).

PRAYER

T HE NEWS from the doctor was not good, Lord. What will become of me? What does the future hold? What will happen to those close to me? Will you be there when I need you? Will you walk—as you have promised—through the valley of the shadow of death with me, or will I have to tread that path alone? Do not desert me. Keep your word. Fulfill your promises. Keep my feet from stumbling. Give me strength to run what is left of my race unafraid. Then in your time, receive me into your eternal presence.

WHEN DEATH DRAWS NEAR

READING

"I WILL NEVER accept the verdict," Hank told himself. "I will fight it tooth and nail every step of the way. I refuse to give in or give up. Did I hear the test results correctly? Maybe I misunderstood the doctor," he thought to himself, "but that haunting word *positive* will not go away. I went to the doctor kicking and screaming in the first place. I told her that nothing was wrong. Doctors make mistakes, you know," Hank continued to argue with himself. "But what if she is right? What if the diagnosis is accurate? Can I ever accept that? Or is this just a terrible nightmare, a bad dream that I will wake up from and everything will be okay?"

PRAYER

THE WORD STICKS in my throat, Lord. Death. How I fear it. How I wish it would go away. Death is my companion now and I need your help to face it. It is the first thing I think of when I wake up, and it is my last thought before I fall asleep. It lies across my path like a newly fallen tree, blocking my way, and I cannot will it away. Help me come to terms with it. Help me treasure each day that I have left as a precious gift from you. Assure me by your mighty resurrection that death is nothing more than the gate to eternal life. Then let me die without fear but in solid confidence and hope.

ON THE DEATH OF A BELOVED

READING

THEY HAD BEEN high school sweethearts, voted "cutest couple" as seniors. Where so many marriages that started out in the teen years had failed, their relationship seemed to grow stronger year by year. They raised three children—two boys and a girl—and now they were enjoying their four grandkids and looking for more to come. But that was not to be. An embolism in a key artery had snuffed out her life and he felt as limp as a wet rag, standing by her casket. He did not know which was worse—the numbness that felt like a dull endless ache or the sharp stabs of grief. In either case, he kept asking himself, "How will I ever get along without her?"

PRAYER

I ALWAYS KNEW this day would come, Lord, I just did not expect it to come so soon. We had plans for the future. We had dreams. We had so much to look forward to—but now the one I loved with all my heart lies in a casket and I stand here limp, weak, helpless, vulnerable, empty. Release me from my deep despair and point out once again how you have conquered death for good. Make today Easter. Share your victory with me. Do not let me cave in to my fears and my loss, but strengthen me with your lively word of hope. Lift me, Lord, lift me high.

PART TWO

PRAYERS FROM
THE HEART

WHEN LIFE IS GOOD

READING

A TRAINER AT the Disney Institute in Orlando, Florida, was asked if Disney employees were rewarded monetarily for their good suggestions. Her response was swift and strong: "Money is a drug." Jesus often warned that money and the things it can buy can easily come between us and his gracious love. The question I need to ask is, "Who is in control of my life? My money or my Lord?" I need to ask this question especially when life is good.

PRAYER

I T IS EASY to forget you, Lord, when life is good, the stock market is climbing, my career is on track, I have good health, and my relationships are all sound. Why is that, Lord? How can I take it all for granted when you are the giver of every good gift? Let me never become so distracted by the so-called good things in life that there is no room for you. Remind me daily of your goodness that I may praise your name forever.

FOR GRATITUDE

READING

THE TERRORIST ATTACK on the World Trade Center and the Pentagon was a tragedy of enormous dimensions. The unspeakable horror tore at our hearts and filled our lives with great sorrow. The response of people across the country was unprecedented. If that same energy and concern could be harnessed on behalf of the hungry of the world, it would make a significant difference in their perilous lives.

Comparing the statistics is a sobering exercise. On 9/11, four jet airplanes were used by terrorists as guided missiles against stationary targets. The loss of life was staggering. And yet, in effect 50 full 747 jumbo jets crash each day in an ongoing daily tragedy. The people represented by this example are victims of hunger and hunger-related conditions. It is a situation that cries out for people with grateful hearts to God for all his benefits to us and a burning desire to seek justice for our sisters and brothers in need.

PRAYER

M AKE ME a grateful person, Lord. Give me a sense of wonder at this magnificent world you called into being by your mighty word. Remind me that none of my possessions ultimately belong to me, but all are on loan from you. Call me to a responsible use of this world's finite resources. Bring to my attention the needs of the poor who struggle for survival when I am so richly blessed. Curb my appetite for more and teach me the joy of sharing. Let all people find happiness and fulfillment living in this world you created. Call me to serve humbly my sisters and brothers in need, seeing Jesus in every person I meet.

FOR FORGIVENESS

READING

CREATE IN ME a clean heart, O God; and renew a right spirit within me. Cast me not away from thy presence; and take not thy holy spirit from me. Restore unto me the joy of thy salvation; and uphold me with thy free spirit.

— Psalm 51:10–12 (KJV)

PRAYER

M Y SOUL IS heavy with guilt, Lord. I have fallen far short of what it means to be your child. I have let down those closest to me, and, in failing them, I have failed you. I cannot shake this feeling of regret. I need your forgiveness, Jesus, friend of sinners. You died to restore me to you and us to one another. In your mercy, remove every stain. Wash me thoroughly and make me wholly yours once more.

FOR GOD'S PRESENCE

READING

TAKING LIFE one day at a time had never been easy for Maggie, but now it was a matter of life and death. She had come within a hair's breadth of losing everything that mattered to her—her marriage, her family, her job. Fortunately, Irene, her closest friend since childhood, got through to her and helped Maggie face up to the truth about her life—that she was an alcoholic and in great need of help. Maggie went through a 12-step treatment program and was learning how to trust God for the first time in her life. Each day of sobriety, hard fought though it was, brought her new hope. With God's help, she knew she could hang in there.

PRAYER

PURSUE ME with your spirit, Lord, that I may be wholly yours. Reach across the divide that my sin has caused and gently lift me to yourself. Let me know you are present in the midst of my struggles, out front, charging ahead into the future you devise in your love for me. Block every fear that would cause me to doubt you. Oppose every evil force that would seek to pry me away from you. Thwart every foul ambition from within that would seek to replace you as my Lord and my God. Let me never be so overwhelmed by my problems nor so terrorized by the future that I lose you, Lord of my life and God of my soul.

WHEN AT A CROSSROADS

READING

"WWJD" READ THE BRACELET David always wore. He started wearing it in college and he found that the simple slogan "What Would Jesus Do?" helped him make decisions—both large and small. But now he was faced with the biggest decision of his life. His company had just offered him a job in a distant community. It would be a big step up in his career path. While it would mean an increase in salary plus several added perks, it would also mean longer hours and added stress. It would involve moving his young family some distance from their hometown to a distant city where they did not know anyone. While David's parents and in-laws were in good health at the present time, David could not count on that forever. Who would watch out for them if ill health struck? David was torn. What would Jesus do? His boss wanted an answer by Monday.

PRAYER

I FIND MYSELF at a crossroads, Lord. I need to make a decision and I need your guidance. As I weigh the pluses and minuses, the positives and negatives, the benefits and drawbacks of each possibility, guide me by your Spirit. Show me the way you would have me go. Give me wisdom and insight, courage and daring, fortitude and conviction, that my decision may advance your name and be best for all whom my decision will affect. Then, grant me the faith and serenity to follow through. Empower me to walk in your footsteps, Jesus.

WHEN GOING THROUGH CHANGE

READING

CHANGE ALWAYS carries with it a measure of worry since we do not ever know for certain what the outcome will be. In fact, the end result may be radically different from what we envisioned when we started. Change carries with it questions such as:

- What will life be like when the change has been made?
- Will it be better?
- Or worse?
- What are the costs, both visible and hidden?

A mature faith learns to trust that God works through all the changes of our lives for our ultimate good, and it leaves outcomes in God's hands.

PRAYER

C HANGE IS a part of life, people say. I know that, Lord, but change troubles me still. I feel as if I am in a high-wire act at the circus. I have let go of one trapeze and am flying in midair, reaching for the next one. I worry about outcomes. I wonder what will become of me. I fear what might happen in this interval between here and there. Catch me, gentle Savior. Let me trust your larger purpose for my life. Strengthen my resolve to follow where you lead. And assure me that when I have reached the destination, you will be there just as you have promised.

FOR SOMEONE WHO WILL LISTEN
READING

THE GREATEST NEED people have today is not for someone who will solve their problems for them, but rather for someone who will listen empathetically to the darkest and deepest wounds of their inner selves. We may feel as though we were useless and not particularly helpful to a friend in the midst of a crisis, and yet he or she will say in gratitude, "You were there when I needed you."

PRAYER

I NEED A FRIEND, Lord, someone who will just listen. Not someone who will try to fix me or attempt to solve my problems, but someone who will accept me for who I am. Not someone who will become anxious, suspicious, or frightened when I share the deepest feelings of my soul, but someone who will accept me. Not someone who will give chatty advice or scold or judge me, but someone who will quietly point me to you. I need someone to listen, Lord, someone like you.

AT A FAMILY REUNION

READING

S UE HAD RESISTED attending their family reunion, held every three years on Hal and Leona's farm. It brought back too many bad memories of growing up—of rivalry with her siblings and of competition for their parents' attention. But now, as she grew older, those ties became more important and, even though she knew she would have to endure Uncle Frank's merciless teasing, she was glad that she had come this time. Hearing all the old stories that were retold every three years somehow grounded her and made her feel like a full person again.

PRAYER

YOU HAVE BROUGHT US together, Lord, from east and west, north and south, unique individuals who share a common story and ancestry, branches from the same trunk. Bless this precious time that we have together. Give us both laughter and tears as we reminisce, and draw us at last into that one family that celebrates your story in eternal splendor.

ON THE BIRTH/ADOPTION OF A CHILD
READING

THEY NEVER forgot that exhilarating moment when their new baby was placed into their arms for the first time, their very own child! How much they had longed for this day. How deeply they had tried to imagine what it would be like and how wide of the mark their anticipation had been from the real thing. Tears running down their cheeks, all they could say over and over was, "Thank you, God. Thank you for this baby."

PRAYER

THANK YOU, Lord, for your gift of this child. Do not let us ever forget the miracle that this child is. Make us wise and patient parents. Help us mold our child after your likeness, following in your pathways. Guard and keep our little one safe from all harm and danger. Be a constant companion and watch over her [or him] all through life. Keep her [or him] faithful to you that at life's end she [or he] may be received into your eternal realm.

BEFORE SURGERY

READING

S UE WAS LYING on the gurney in the holding area waiting to be rolled into surgery. She could feel the cold of the IV fluids dripping into her arm. The presurgical nurses had completed all their preparation work and had moved on to prep other patients for surgery. Now Sue lay there alone with her thoughts—and her fears. Despite the assurances of her surgeon and her confidence in his skills and knowledge, she was aware that there are always things that can go wrong. How much she wished this ordeal were over and done with. Suddenly, the double doors leading into the surgical suite opened and she felt the orderly wheeling her inside. "God be with me," she whispered.

PRAYER

G O WITH ME into surgery, Lord. Watch over me while I am unconscious and keep me in your protective care. Grant to the surgical team wisdom and skill, good judgment and courage, and by your gracious will, bring healing. I am your servant. I trust in you and will praise your righteous name forever.

FOR THE PEOPLE OF THE CHURCH
READING

THE CHURCH'S one foundation
Is Jesus Christ, her Lord;
She is his new creation
By water and the Word.
From heav'n he came and sought her
To be his holy bride;
With his own blood he bought her,
And for her life he died.[1]

— Samuel J. Stone, 1839–1900

1 "The Church's One Foundation," hymn 369, stanza 1, from *Lutheran Book of Worship* (Minneapolis: Augsburg Publishing House, 1978).

PRAYER

L IVING GOD, in our baptism you united us with Christ and named us servants in your church. Bind our hearts together in a true community of love. Renew us in faith and commitment. May your Holy Spirit empower us to be faithful disciples, using the gifts you have entrusted to us to serve others and give glory to your name through blatant acts of kindness and reckless deeds of compassion. Be with all pastors and people that in a strong unity of purpose we might share your life and be a beacon of hope in a dark and loveless world.

FOR ALL PEOPLE

READING

[THE LORD] SHALL JUDGE between the nations,
and shall arbitrate for many peoples;
they shall beat their swords into plowshares,
and their spears into pruning hooks;
nation shall not lift up sword against nation,
neither shall they learn war any more.

— Isaiah 2:4 (NRSV)

PRAYER

B RING RESOLUTION, Lord, to the struggles and fears of all people. Let them know your perfect peace. Be with all who carry heavy burdens of anguish and hurt, stress and anxiety, disappointment and distress. Let them find relief in the gentle rain of your ever-present care. Comfort the dying, fill the hungry with sufficient food, and uphold the whole human race, imbuing all people with a spirit of mutual care, concern, and cooperation. Mold the hearts of people everywhere on the template of Jesus' love that wars might cease. Let the prophet's vision prevail. May all nations forsake their weapons of mass destruction and death. So urge them onward that they beat their swords into plowshares, ending their warring madness, once and for all. Grant it, Lord, peace in our time.

FOR JUSTICE AND PEACE

READING

LET THERE be peace on earth
And let it begin with me;
Let there be peace on earth,
The peace that was meant to be.

With God, our Creator,
Family all are we.
Let us walk with each other
In perfect harmony.

Let peace begin with me,
Let this be the moment now.
With every step I take,
Let this be my joyous vow.

To take each moment
And live each moment
In peace eternally.
Let there be peace on earth
And let it begin with me.[1]

— Sy Miller and Jill Jackson

PRAYER

I T IS NOT YOUR WILL, Lord, that any of your children should lack the basic necessities of life—food, safe drinking water, clothing, or shelter. Work justice in all the earth. Be the safe place for the fearful. Bring peace and stability to all those places in the world that are torn by conflict and war. Be with the victims of natural disasters and support them as they attempt to put their shattered lives back together again. Work on my heart, Lord, that I might see other people through your eyes. Fill me with compassion and empathy for all who hurt. Empower me to bring comfort and hope into the aching corners of their lives. Let there be peace on earth, Lord, and let it begin with me.

THE PRAYER OF ST. FRANCIS

READING

H E WAS BORN in the Italian city of Assisi in 1182 to wealth and privilege. As a young man Francis dreamed of being a soldier. He was attracted to what he saw as the glamour and romance of warfare. But the reality was something altogether different. He was captured and made a prisoner of war in his first battle. Struck with illness that nearly took his life, he was released and sent home to recover. There he renounced his wealth and sought to emulate Jesus' life of poverty. He gathered a band of followers that became an order of brothers bearing his name. They wandered throughout Italy. He rebuilt churches and taught simplicity of life, love of all creatures, and concern for lepers and the poor. The following prayer has been traditionally credited to St. Francis's authorship but that cannot be authenticated. It does, however, reflect his teachings.

PRAYER

LORD, MAKE ME an instrument of your peace.
Where there is hatred, let me sow love;
Where there is injury, pardon;
Where there is discord, union;
Where there is doubt, faith;
Where there is despair, hope;
Where there is darkness, light;
Where there is sadness, joy.
Grant that I may not so much seek
To be consoled as to console;
To be understood as to understand;
To be loved as to love.
For it is in giving that we receive;
It is in pardoning that we are pardoned; and
It is in dying that we are born to eternal life.

— attributed to St. Francis of Assisi, 1182–1226

PART THREE

TIMES AND
SEASONS

IN WINTER

READING

THE GLOOM and dejection that people often feel during the long winter months, particularly in northern climates, has a name. It is a disease called Seasonal Affective Disorder, or SAD for short, an apt acronym. For those who suffer this malady, its arrival each year is as predictable as the icy wind that rattles the windows and chills to the bone. It's brought on by lack of light, and a simple cure is effected by adding light in the same wavelengths as the sun's rays. We are made to be creatures of the light, not the dark.

PRAYER

THE DAYS ARE SHORT and the nights long now, Lord. Snow covers the earth as far as the eye can see, hiding the flowers and the grass under a dull gray blanket. The laughter of children on their saucers hurtling down the hills just mocks my gloom. Leaden skies and barren trees drive away what little creativity I have. Hope dissipates like the clouds that form and scatter when I breathe the frigid night air. Stand by me, Lord. Remind me that this darkness will pass. Tide me over until spring warms the earth and awakens the slumbering crocus and sleeping forsythia from their long winter naps. Remind me of your resurrection, vivid sign of your power over death. Let me see the springtime of your love even now in the dead of winter. Be my light, gracious friend, that I might bloom and live to your glory.

IN SPRING

READING

T HE DOORBELL RANG, rousing Jack Collins from his favorite family room chair where he had dozed off. On the porch step stood one of the neighborhood children, armed with a box of chocolate candy bars. "Would you like to buy a candy bar for my youth league baseball team, Mr. Collins?" asked the child.

"Of course," Jack said, thinking to himself, *It must be spring.*

PRAYER

F OR GENTLE BREEZES that rustle the fresh new leaves of trees, for crabapple blooms and rolling meadows carpeted in yellow, and for dandelion seeds that invite little children to blow and scatter them ~~with squeals of delight,~~ I give you praise, Lord God.

For longer days and warm air, for the reawakening of creation, for the promise of new life and every new beginning, I praise your glory, good Creator.

For every opportunity to serve, for the good news of your grace, for every sign of your power to make things new, I offer a paean of praise.

For spring, I give you thanks, O Lord.

IN SUMMER

READING

J ACK COLLINS found it strange. How much he missed the joyous sounds through the open windows of children pouring out of their school bus when it pulled up to the stop in front of his house and deposited its precious cargo. But it was summer now and school was out. The children were scattered at babysitters, nurseries, day camps, and other places their parents left them while they worked. In the evening when it began to cool off they could be seen roaming the neighborhood—adolescent girls and boys pretending not to notice each other. "How much things change and still stay the same," Jack Collins thought to himself. "There must be a parable here."

PRAYER

THE BALMY DAYS of spring have given way to the blast furnace that is summer, Lord. The heat and humidity conspire to intensify my discomfort. Send gentle breezes and cooling rain. Water the parched earth, Lord, and stir within me a strong desire to serve you, O God of my life. Let each day be dedicated to you. Fill me with your spirit that I might find my sole delight in serving you until that glorious day when I shall dwell with you in eternal sunshine.

IN AUTUMN

READING

F OR EVERYTHING there is a season, and a time for every matter under heaven:

> a time to be born, and a time to die;
>
> a time to plant, and a time to pluck up what is planted.

— Ecclesiastes 3:1–2 (NRSV)

PRAYER

I T IS AUTUMN, Lord, and where I live the trees have become your canvas. You splash colors across the wooded hills—brilliant red on the sumac, bright orange on the sugar maple, deep yellow on the elm and locust—a cacophony of color, all singing your praise, my Creator. At the same time the rich-hued landscape brings to mind the end of things, and harvest—a time to pluck up, as the Teacher says. As the leaves of summer erupt in a riot of color and then fall lifeless to the ground, so remind me that my days are numbered, that life on this planet does not last forever, but that you rule for all time and all eternity—and your rule is good. Remind me and renew my faith, O God of nature.

PRAYING THE HOURS

F OR CENTURIES, members of religious orders have maintained regular, formal times for prayer called the Daily Office. Some of these prayers have been passed down over the centuries and some are of more recent vintage. Over time they have acquired a sheen and cadence that make them absolute gems of Christian prayer.

Lauds is a prayer of praise when you first awake.

Prime is the Office appointed for the first hour, which is traditionally 6:00 A.M.

Terce is a prayer for the third hour, or 9:00 A.M.

Sext is the sixth hour prayer, prayed at noon.

Nones, the ninth hour, is for midafternoon, 3:00 P.M.

Vespers is the prayer after supper, or evening prayers.

Compline is the last prayer of the day, at bedtime.

PRAYER

L ORD, I WOULD MAKE my whole day a conversation with you. From my first awaking through to closing eyes for nighttime rest, let me turn to you as my companion. I am eager to be part of whatever you have in store for me, Lord, and I know that talking to you about it all the time will make me more alert to the possibilities you throw my way and the people you put in my path. Talk to me, Lord, and I will listen.

LAUDS (WHEN YOU AWAKE)

PRAYER

YOU SENT a little bird to wake me, Lord. Outside my window it sang my sleep away and chirped of your goodness. May its joyful song propel me into a day of praise for all the wonders you have done for me, that I may claim your promises for my life this whole day through.

PRIME (WHEN YOU ARISE)

PRAYER

T HANK YOU for the morning, Lord.

For sunshine and the promise of new possibilities for serving, I give you praise.

Watch over me the whole day long, that at day's end I might rest securely in your protective care.

TERCE (MIDMORNING)

PRAYER

L ORD GOD, you have called your servants to ventures of which we cannot see the ending, by paths as yet untrodden, through perils unknown. Give us faith to go out with good courage, not knowing where we go, but only that your hand is leading us and your love supporting us; through Jesus Christ our Lord. Amen.[1]

---

1 From *Lutheran Book of Worship* (Minneapolis: Augsburg Publishing House, 1978), p. 137.

SEXT (NOON)

PRAYER

I T'S THE MIDDLE of the day, Lord, the halfway point. All that has gone before is past and cannot be reclaimed. All that lies ahead waits to happen. Where I have gone off course, forgive and restore—and what you intend, empower, that at day's end I may look back, and, from the vantage point of time, have reason to rejoice.

NONES (MIDAFTERNOON)

PRAYER

THE SUN is leaning into evening, Lord, yet, in your loving-kindness, you provide time to serve you still. Send someone my way, Lord, someone who needs your gentle touch. Let that someone feel it from you through me.

VESPERS (EVENING PRAYER)

PRAYER

This prayer was written in the fifth century . . .

O GOD, FROM WHOM COME all holy desires, all good counsels, and all just works, give to us, your servants, that peace which the world cannot give, that our hearts may be set to obey your commandments; and also that we, being defended from the fear of our enemies, may live in peace and quietness; through the merits of Jesus Christ our Savior, who lives and reigns with you and the Holy Spirit, God forever. Amen.

COMPLINE (BEDTIME PRAYER)

PRAYER

This prayer was written by John Henry Newman, English writer and philosopher (1801–1890).

O LORD, SUPPORT US all the day long of this troubled life, until the shadows lengthen and the evening comes and the busy world is hushed, the fever of life is over, and our work is done. Then, Lord, in your mercy, grant us a safe lodging and a holy rest, and peace at the last; through Jesus Christ our Lord. Amen.

MATINS (IF WAKEFUL
IN THE EARLY MORNING)

PRAYER

T HANK YOU for the night, Lord.

For shadows and the promise of healing sleep, I give you praise.

Watch over me the whole night long, that at night's end I might wake refreshed and serve you anew.

ADVENT

READING

O GOD, OUR HELP in ages past,
Our hope for years to come,
Our shelter from the stormy blast,
And our eternal home.[1]

— Isaac Watts, 1674–1748

---

1 "O God, Our Help in Ages Past," hymn 320, stanza 1, from *Lutheran Book of Worship* (Minneapolis: Augsburg Publishing House, 1978).

PRAYER

A NEW CHURCH YEAR, Lord, and like all of creation I await your coming. Thanks and praise to you, O God, for your gracious favor upon all your people; for goodness undeserved and gifts no one can number; for life and health and loving friends; for work and leisure; for all good things you freely give; but, more than anything else, for Jesus Christ, who lifts the hopes of all your people and leads them in your ways. I offer up praise to you, O God, for every sign of his presence in my life—and for your life-giving Spirit who calls me to faith. Deliver me from every evil that gets in the way of your saving purpose, and in this year now aborning let the world know peace; yes, let us know peace in our time, God of the ages.

CHRISTMAS

READING AND PRAYER

Ah, dearest Jesus, holy Child,

Make Thee a bed, soft, undefiled,

Within my heart, that it may be

A quiet chamber kept for Thee.[1]

— Martin Luther (1535)

ALMIGHTY GOD, you sent angels to announce the birth of your Son. Let me receive him with great joy and much thanksgiving. Let me make a home within my heart for him, this gentle child of promise. In the beauty of the Christmas season bring to my remembrance his embrace of the lost and hurting, the outcast and marginalized, the hungry and oppressed. Give me a compassionate heart and a conscience-driven thirst for justice that responds in helpful ways to all who hurt in any way in any corner of the world. Grant this, great Giver, in the holy name of Mary's son, Jesus my Savior.

1 "From Heaven Above to Earth I Come," stanza 13, hymn 85, *The Lutheran Hymnal* (St. Louis: Concordia Publishing House, 1941).

EPIPHANY

READING AND PRAYER

I N THE TIME of King Herod, after Jesus was born in Bethlehem of Judea, wise men from the East came to Jerusalem, asking, "Where is the child who has been born king of the Jews? For we observed his star at its rising, and have come to pay him homage."

— Matthew 2:1–2 (NRSV)

Magi from the east came to pay you tribute, Lord. They were truly a wonder to behold—so wise in the meaning and movements of the stars, so gullible in their encounter with those in power, so exotic in their appearance, so willing to follow when an alternate route home was offered, so joyful to meet you in your crib, and so generous with the gifts they gave. Strengthen me too in faith that, kneeling at your cradle, I might rise to serve you and do your will.

LENT

B ENEATH THE CROSS of Jesus
I long to take my stand;
The shadow of a mighty rock
Within a weary land,
A home within a wilderness,
A rest upon the way,
From the burning of the noontide heat
And burdens of the day.

— Elizabeth C. Clephane, 1830–1869

PRAYER

O CHRIST, LAMB OF GOD, you take away the sin of the world, have mercy upon me.

O Christ, Lamb of God, you take away the sin of the world, have mercy upon me.

O Christ, Lamb of God, you take away the sin of the world, grant me your peace.

EASTER

READING

THINE IS THE GLORY, Risen, conqu'ring Son;
Endless is the vict'ry Thou o'er death hast won!
Angels in bright raiment Rolled the stone away,
Kept the folded graveclothes Where thy body lay.
Thine is the glory, Risen, conqu'ring Son;
Endless is the vict'ry Thou o'er death hast won![1]

— Edmond Budry, 1854–1932

---

1 "Thine Is the Glory," stanza 1, hymn 145, from *Lutheran Book of Worship* (Minneapolis: Augsburg Publishing House, 1978).

PRAYER

C HRIST, HAVING BEEN RAISED from the dead, you will die no more. Death has no more power over you. On this happy day, I pool my praise with all your people of every time and every place. On this day you forever broke the stranglehold of sin and death over human lives. By the glorious light of Easter you forever banished darkness from the lives of your people. Shine, Easter light, illumine all the earth with the brightness of your eternal radiance.

PENTECOST

READING

O DAY FULL OF GRACE that now we see
Appearing on earth's horizon,
Bring light from our God that we may be
Replete in his joy this season.
God, shine for us now in this dark place;
Your name on our hearts emblazon.[1]

— Nikolai F. S. Grundtvig, 1783–1872

1 "O Day Full of·Grace," stanza 1, hymn 161, from *Lutheran Book of Worship* (Minneapolis: Augsburg Publishing House, 1978).

PRAYER

O SPIRIT OF THE LIVING GOD, you are a consuming fire. Unleash your power. Bend my will to yours that I might gladly carry out deeds of mercy and kindness in your name. Surge within the lives of your people. Kindle within us the fire of your love. Make us to be a people alive with your gospel, on fire for every good work in your name. May others see our love and be drawn to you. Be in my heart, Lord. Now is the time.